NAFTA, GATT and the World Trade Organization:
The New Rules for Corporate Conquest

By Kristin Dawkins

COUNTERING THE CORPORATE ORDER

It's called the World Trade Organization—a brand new institution designed to manage a world order based on corporate control of the planet's productive and reproductive rights. It is the crowning achievement of the Uruguay Round negotiations of the GATT, the General Agreement on Tariffs and Trade. Under the World Trade Organization each member country "shall ensure the conformity of its law, regulations and administrative procedures with its obligations as provided" in the new rules of the GATT. The World Trade Organization—or WTO—will have what they call "legal personality," as much authority in other words as the United Nations or the World Bank. One of its goals is "to achieve greater coherence in global economic policy-making" in tandem with the World Bank and the International Monetary Fund, says the founding document. However, the founding document makes no reference at all to the United Nations. The net result is that the nations of the world will have less and less of a voice in determining their economic futures.

Likewise, the North American Free Trade Agreement (NAFTA) establishes new international laws that can neutralize or override a given country's democratically enacted policies. Both the Uruguay Round of GATT and NAFTA arm transnational corporations with unprecedented political power. Both are the legacy of the Reagan-Bush agenda to "liberalize" trade and deregulate investment. Both were supported and finalized by President Clinton. Without the capacity to manage economic and financial flows, many countries, the United States included, will experience worsening deficits, skyrocketing unemployment and ecological catastrophe. Only by stopping the "free trade" agenda can we preserve the opportunity in countries all over the world to develop alternative models for rebuilding communities.

We came very close to stopping the NAFTA in November 1993. Nationwide organizing among labor and environmentalists, consumers, farmers and others produced the most powerful and popular coalition this country has seen in decades. Up until a few days before the final vote on NAFTA in the U.S. Congress, it looked like a majority of the House of Representatives would vote "NO," thanks to grass-roots pressure nationwide. However, in a revealing display of the democratic process in America, the

Clinton Administration persuaded a couple dozen legislators to switch their votes at the last minute by promising them billions of dollars worth of "pork," as it's called. Conservative columnist George Will wrote on November 11 that "votes are for sale and the President is buying."

Ralph Nader's office prepared a nice list showing that the pork included contracts for six C-17 military cargo planes for Texas representative Eddie Bernice Johnson, scaling back proposed cigarette taxes for North Carolina Representative Charlie Rose, allowing vegetables to continue being saturated with the cancer-causing, ozone-depleting pesticide methyl bromide for several Floridian congresspersons, delays in cleaning up the Boston Harbor, financing for the construction of new bridges and trade centers, aircraft carriers, and so on.

Although Congress voted 234-200 in favor of NAFTA on November 17, the coalition's efforts were not in vain. The American public saw how our democratic process really works and we learned which congresspeople cannot be relied upon under political pressure from the White House. We learned how trade negotiations affect jobs, health, and the environment and how our economy is linked with that of Mexico and other countries. Organized labor learned about environmental issues and environmentalists learned about labor rights. Members of consumer organizations learned how food safety is jeopardized by federal farm policy and farmers found friends in the consumer movement. Activists from the United States formed alliances with activists from Mexico and Canada. Now we must build upon this experience to sustain a grass-roots national movement that can effectively collaborate with international partners to fight for a sensible economic development strategy—one that I characterize as community-based instead or corporate-based, even in the context of the global economy.

THE PRODUCTIVE AND REPRODUCTIVE SECTOR

Third World critics of free trade are very advanced in terms of devising alternatives to the corporate order. I'm not talking about utopian scenarios, but practical scenarios to ensure that community-based economic and political systems can continue to function. In the heart of the industrialized world, it sometimes is difficult to imagine what the alternative scenarios might look like. We stand to learn much from people in communities elsewhere in the world.

A community-based model for economic development is grounded in an understanding of the *productive* and *reproductive rights of the planet*. By productive rights, I mean productivity in the sense of the economy, labor force, plants and technology that yield the gross domestic product. By reproductive rights I mean the ecology of the planet, the natural resources that exist, the biotic systems that enable life to continue, and the way in which humans interact with the environment. In both areas, the productive and reproductive sectors, the corporate agenda seeks to gain control over resources. We as a community movement, on the other hand, are trying to maintain or regain community

Kristin Dawkins

With Resistance Notes By
Jeremy Brecher

GATT, NAFTA & WTO
The Emerging New World Order

Kristin Dawkins is a Senior Fellow at the Institute of Agriculture and Trade Policy. She worked for 16 years in community development and public policy research in Philadelphia, including 9 years as the executive director of the Philadelphia Jobs in Energy Project. She has a Master's Degree in city planning from M.I.T.

Jeremy Brecher is a historian and co-editor of *Global Visions: Beyond the New World Order* (South End Press, 1993)

This pamphlet is printed entirely on acid-free recycled paper.

Pamphlet Series Publishers
Greg Ruggiero and Stuart Sahulka

Pamphlet #29
Open Magazine Pamphlet Series
First Printing • April 1994

ISBN: 1-884519-04-0

OPEN MAGAZINE
PAMPHLET SERIES
P.O. Box 2726
Westfield, New Jersey 07091-2726
Tel: (908) 789-9608 **Fax:** (908) 654-3829
E-Mail: opengrss@maestro.com

LETTER FROM THE PUBLISHERS

"Why is everyone so quiet?
Is this the Democracy you wanted?"—The Zapatistas

March 1994

Dear Friends,

We have interrupted our production schedule on this and several other new pamphlets and projects in order to publish ZAPATISTAS: SPREADING HOPE FOR GRASSROOTS CHANGE, STARTING FROM CHIAPAS. We have rushed to get out these titles in solidarity with the struggle for authentic democracy and land reform in Mexico. As the Zapatista struggle is still in-progress, expressions of support coming from progressive communities in Mexico, the United States and Canada have meaningful impact. The time to stand up and speak out is *now*.

The Zapatista insurgency is sending a wake-up call to North Americans from Chiapas to the Arctic Circle. They wake us up to the fact that the destinies of the peoples of Mexico, Canada, and the United States are inextricably bound to one another. They wake us up to the fact that "NAFTA is a death sentence" for indigenous communities, and that what is at stake is not only the obvious erosion of democratic rights, but survival itself. We must express our solidarity with indigenous peoples now making a move to protect their survival and exert meaningful sovereignty. And we must express solidarity by challenging the two-wing business party and the brainless media that supports it here in the United States.

The Zapatistas ask us to come together in resistance to unregulated power and the illegitimate democracy that NAFTA imposes on North Americans and that GATT imposes on the world. They challenge us, as individuals and communities, to find workable alternatives to a society based on conquest, commercialism, domination and control.

The question is, what can we actually do? While it seems ridiculous to call for an insurgency movement here in the States, it's even more ridiculous to accept the emerging new world order. As individuals and organizations, students and teachers, artists and activists, readers and listeners, women and men, indigenous, black and white, gay and straight, inner city and rural, academy and street; tribe, community, comrades and kin, we must reach out to one another in solidarity and resistance.

If debased, profit-sick corporations can come together and agree on a GATT, a WTO, and a NAFTA, we in the independent community can launch agreements and coalitions of resistance. *Now* is the time to form solidarities, build bridges, vocalize, and mobilize. We can begin by speaking out in the public spaces of our everyday lives: in the progressive press, in the classroom, in the library, on the Internet, over the airwaves and in the street.

The depravity of corporations is their need to dominate and homogenize. In such a landscape, our differences are our power. Let's use it. We, the public, are already everywhere.

With Hope & Solidarity,

Greg Ruggiero & Stuart Sahulka,
The Publishers

control over those resources. Who but the communities which have lived with them for millennia, until the present Western model of development began to encroach, understand what the reproductive thresholds of a particular ecological system really are?

When you look at the famine in Somalia, or at any number of other communities that are in deep crisis, you can usually trace the reasons for that trouble back to the intervention of the Western mode of development. The Somalis were originally a nomadic people. What are called "warlords" in the media are actually tribal leaders of peoples who roamed throughout their territory. They had a particular lifestyle that existed in accord with the kinds of land and water resources that existed there. However, when the global economic system entered the picture, the indigenous social order was disrupted and quickly destroyed. Traditional agriculture systems in Somalia and elsewhere were displaced and eventually destroyed by corporate agribusiness which produces cash crops for exports, crops that the indigenous people in those communities cannot even eat. The cash crops, in turn, generate foreign exchange that is used to pay off debts to the World Bank, or to private banking institutions. In the end, virtually none of the profit derived from the natural resources of these countries goes back to the people. Their agriculture system becomes a cash crop, a variable in an equation controlled by the international banking industry.

To survive under corporate agribusiness control, the people then need to either purchase imported food or, in many cases, starvation ensues—in part because nomads and peasants lack cash to purchase foods and in part because cash crops are grown as monocultures based on single varieties of seed requiring extensive land use and chemicals, which destroy the soil and its biotic ecosystems. At that point people become unable to grow even subsistence levels of food for their own families. This is the cycle responsible for the desertification throughout Africa. It's also the cycle disrupting social systems that function in a very different context than what we think of as the Western social order. As a result, we have famine and war spreading throughout the planet.

HISTORY BEHIND GATT

In this century, the GATT and the other Bretton Woods institutions—the World Bank and the International Monetary Fund—have been the main instigators of these kinds of patterns. They're called the Bretton Woods institutions because they were designed in a small New Hampshire town by that name. The world's financial elite convened there back in 1944. Their ostensible purpose was to help Europe and avoid a repetition of the conditions that led to World War II. The less ostensible but more valid interpretation of their interest in rebuilding Europe was that the United States still had a highly industrialized infrastructure producing products for which we did not have consumers. Rebuilding Europe was essentially part of a plan to increase markets for the U.S. productive sector.

Formalized in 1948, GATT is now an agreement among more than 100 countries, each of which, in theory, has equal power in negotiating the rules of global trade in resources and finished products. The seeming equality of participation of membership in GATT is actually an illusion. The power of decision making resides with those countries that have the largest market share for whichever product is being negotiated. U.S.-based transnational corporations control approximately 70 percent of grains worldwide. This means that when the United States starts negotiating food policy with other countries, if the other countries are importing and dependent upon us for their food supply, then they have no real political leverage with which to negotiate.

THE URUGUAY ROUND

Over the years, from 1948 to today, GATT has gone through a lot of negotiated changes. Negotiators for the Clinton Administration and Europe finally worked out a number of compromises to conclude the very controversial eighth round, called the Uruguay Round after the country in which it was started in 1986. With the creation of the World Trade Organization (WTO), if the U.S. Congress and other countries' congresses or parliaments endorse it, the very nature of trade policymaking will change. One likely change is that national decision-making processes to approve or disapprove new trade policies will disappear. Instead, the creation of international laws affecting trade-related economic, environmental, and other social policy will lie in the hands of unaccountable trade bureaucrats.

The Uruguay Round of GATT was encouraged by the chairman of American Express, James Robinson, III, who has since resigned. It was his and Ronald Reagan's initiative back in 1986 that got 108 countries to sit down together at the negotiating table. It is not therefore surprising that one of the proposals in the Uruguay Round was to add "services"—banking, insurance, and so on—to the GATT's authority. Gradually, nations would lose their right to base their economies on domestic banking, insurance, transportation, public utilities, and other critical service sectors. The impact would have been so grave that other countries have, so far, successfully fought off this proposal. Also in the Uruguay Round were proposals to deregulate agriculture in unprecedented ways. This text was drafted by Daniel Amstutz, a vice president of the Cargill Company, one of the biggest agribusiness firms in the world. It's not a coincidence that small farmers worldwide have been in the forefront of opposition to the deregulation of national agriculture polices. In this case, the opponents lost. The new World Trade Organization will enforce the new rules for agriculture which will create the conditions for a global race to the bottom in terms of food prices, food safety, and food quality, and spell the end of policies that promote national food security.

TRIPS, TRIMS AND "TRADE BARRIERS"

The Uruguay Round of negotiations also opened a Pandora's box of non-tariff issues including two that are of special importance to developing countries: TRIPs and TRIMs. TRIPs are *trade-related intellectual property rights* and refer to the rules that would allow companies to strengthen their monopoly of patented intellectual property and new technology. Enforced by the new World Trade Organization, TRIPs inhibit economic development, slow the application of the best available, environment-friendly technologies, and hinder the development of non-resource intensive industries in the Third World. Third World communities are opposed to the double standard in the way TRIPs will be applied. Third World proposals for TRIPs protecting their genetic resources and indigenous technologies were disregarded by the high-tech countries during the Uruguay Round negotiations and will not be recognized by the World Trade Organization.

Trade-related investment measures, called TRIMs, are now in place in many countries, so that when a major corporation comes into the country, the corporation is required to invest in certain areas of the local economy. One such TRIM requirement might be to buy a certain amount of the inputs for a product from the host country, so that there is some trickle down. Another requirement might be to employ a certain number of the country's people, ensuring a degree of job development. There are a wide variety of investment measures that countries impose upon foreign corporations when they come in. With the establishment of the World Trade Organization, however, those TRIMs will become illegal trade barriers. This is all part of the deregulatory regime of the Uruguay Round of GATT. The resulting drain of resources from a national economy to foreign investors will hinder the ability of many countries to promote local development and environmental protection.

From its beginning in the 1940s, GATT dealt mostly with tariffs, which are essentially taxes, on traded manufactured goods. In the intervening rounds it began to address what are called *non-tariff barriers*, the set of rules and regulations that countries impose upon trade. For example, a border inspection is considered a non-tariff barrier because the inspection is not reflected as a tariff on the traded goods. Under the Uruguay Round agreement, countries will be bound to a whole new set of rules that deregulate non-tariff barriers—rules that can override a country's own laws, including environmental regulations. For example, GATT dispute panels have obliged Indonesia to lift its ban on the export of raw logs and obliged Thailand to lift its ban on the import of tobacco—on grounds that these laws were "disguised barriers to trade." From a GATT-level, corporate perspective, another country's environmental regulations restricting the import of products that endanger health and safety or perhaps have been processed in an ecologically unsafe manner may be seen as unacceptable trade restrictions. The tuna-dolphin case probably explains this better than any other example.

THE TUNA DOLPHIN CASE

My family boycotted tuna fish throughout my whole childhood. We participated in a long-term boycott campaign to require companies to use a new type of fishing technique that didn't kill dolphins. After many years, we finally won, and we all began to eat tuna fish again. But Mexico and some other countries didn't have the resources with which to upgrade their fishing boats. They continued to fish with the old fashioned purse seine nets. In many cases, the fishermen lived in rural beach communities, yet when they brought their fish to market they were able to sell into the global trade.

Mexico objected to our Marine Mammal Protection Act, and they used the GATT to do so. They said that our ecological law protecting dolphins was a barrier to their ability to trade in tuna fish. One key principle in the GATT establishes that discrimination between "like products"—tuna fish from one country vs. tuna fish from another country—is "illegal." A new precedent, however, was set in the tuna-dolphin case. That precedent says that *you're not allowed to discriminate on the basis of processes*, specifically. Essentially most ecological measures—whether you're talking about smokestack scrubbers or solar panels—involve alternative production *processes*. But, in this case, tuna caught one way cannot be treated differently, said the GATT dispute-resolution panel, than tuna caught another way.

If the tuna-dolphin case is a precedent, it means that in any number of areas it would become illegal to restrict the import of products that were made with ecologically unsound production methods. Now, if you're a poor, Third World country, you might want to invest in environmental technologies, but you can't afford to. This was one of the big issues at the Earth Summit: whether or not technology transfer would be made possible through international policy. The United States' position was, ABSOLUTELY NOT: technology will be made available at strictly commercial rates.

There is another important item to understand in the tuna-dolphin case. The GATT panel ruling says that *no nation can pass a national law that affects territory beyond its national boundaries*. In the case of tuna fishing, national boundaries are considered to extend for a 200 mile zone into the deep oceans. Because our national law would apply to tuna caught beyond the two hundred mile zone, the GATT panel decided that our national law was unfair.

So, on the one hand, Mexico cannot afford to upgrade its fishing boats. On the other hand, U.S. citizens are denied their right to pass laws banning inhumane products. The solution to this conflict lies in the negotiation of international agreements that enable the transfer of technology and funds, through a variety of tariff and non-tariff mechanisms, to enable small and medium-sized businesses throughout the Third World to invest in upgrading to meet ecological standards, so that a lack of environmental protection does not become a competitive advantage.

Now that the Uruguay Round negotiations are over, there is an effort among many environmentalists to counteract the tuna-dolphin precedent and allow countries to discriminate against goods that are not made with ecologically-sound "production-and-process-methods," a concept newly crowned with its own jargon and acronym—PPMs. The problem is that rules requiring ecologically-sound PPMs could hurt a lot of Third World economies if they are not combined with rules ensuring affordable access to environmental technologies. To make matters worse, PPMs and other trade-related environmental policies are being planned by the 24 wealthiest industrialized countries through the Organization for Economic Cooperation and Development (OECD). While the OECD has invited some input from environmentalists in OECD countries, neither Third World governments nor Third World environmentalists are involved.

INTELLECTUAL PROPERTY AND
THE BIODIVERSITY CONVENTION

The controversy in the tuna-dolphin case was exacerbated by the U.S. position in the Earth Summit negotiations where it was quite clear that our government had no interest whatsoever in making ecological upgrades possible for other countries. Nor was there even an interest in advancing ecological practices here in our own country. Two treaties indicate this quite clearly. The Biodiversity Convention, which ostensibly was intended to protect species, is not really about species. George Bush did not sign this treaty—alone among 156 signatories in Rio de Janeiro—because US negotiators failed to draft a sufficiently strong TRIPS clause. Nevertheless, the treaty does permit biotechnology corporations to declare genes as their private property—a variation on the TRIPs rule of the new WTO.

Declaring genetic matter as corporate property prevents indigenous communities from participating in free trade and profiting from generations of unique cultivation. Transnational corporations introduce genetically-engineered varieties of those plants into the global marketplace and reap all the profit. Corporate scientists visit remote native communities, find out from the local people what plants have medicinal or food value, take samples back to the corporate lab for "engineering" and patent the resulting species as commercial products owned and controlled by the corporation. The community that developed the original material will not only receive zero benefits or royalties for having cultivated a unique species, but now they must actually *purchase* the seeds or derivative medicines to avoid violation of international patents and infringement of GATT laws.

Third World negotiators managed to achieve some rights under the Biodiversity Convention, including clauses that required some compensation be paid by patent-holders to the so-called "country of origin" for a given gene. President Clinton has now signed it, but his administration has made it clear that they will send it to Congress for ratification with an interpretive statement insisting "any access to or transfer of technology that occurs in this agreement recognizes and is consistent with the adequate and effective protection of intellectual property rights," thus strengthening the rights of the biotechnology industry while denying both the intellectual property rights of peasants, farmers and indigenous cultivators of valuable genetic varieties and the financial difficulties of developing countries.

THE CLIMATE CHANGE CONVENTION AND OIL

The Climate Change negotiations had a somewhat different set of interests working. Here, oil companies stood to lose from strong regulations against global warming practices. You may remember that George Bush said he would not attend the Earth Summit in Rio—until the very last week prior to the conference. This was a tactic, a successful strategy which forced the world's industrialized countries to accept weaker treaty terms. Eventually, Bush went and the United States did sign it, but only after watering it down so that countries must merely *aim* to reduce their emissions—with no obligation to really do so under international law. To Bill Clinton's credit, during his first weeks as President he committed his administration to earlier, more stringent terms—a firm commitment to reduce carbon dioxide emissions to 1990 levels by the year 2000. When the Congress rejected his plan to tax energy consumption during partisan battles over his first budget, however, Clinton backed away from these goals.

Indeed, President Clinton's willingness to retreat from the oil-and-gas lobbyists during the first budget fight and his bombing of Iraq immediately upon taking office indicate it will be business-as-usual for the U.S. oil industry. Much of Clinton's foreign policy—especially his militarism—merely continues plans conceived during the Reagan-Bush years. The point is that too many of the foreign policy initiatives that have been promoted as socially, ecologically, or economically for the betterment of humanity are, in reality, just charades intended to increase the access of the largest corporations to other peoples' natural resources.

THE ROLE OF THE MILITARY

We need to question the role of the military in international affairs. If you look at what's happening in the United Nations right now, there are proposals for peacekeeping initiatives billed as humanitarian interventions in a dozen countries. The *Los Angeles Times* ran a report over a year ago showing that *two-thirds of Somalia's territory has been leased out to four oil companies*. Only a few other papers picked up that story, including the *International Herald Tribune* on January 19, 1993. Indeed, with massive budget cuts in the U.N. agencies for social and economic development and increases for "peacekeeping," the United Nations itself threatens to become a military instrument of corporate power.

The current Secretary General of the United Nations, Boutras Ghali, comes from Egypt, the number two client state of the United States, second to Israel. Within two weeks of taking office as George Bush's favorite candidate for the top job at the United Nations, Boutras Ghali eliminated the only agency in the world that was attempting to regulate transnational corporations, the United Nations Center on Transnational Corporations (UNCTC). Now, a much reduced staff relocated to Geneva is called the new Transnational Corporations and Management Division of the United Nations. However, the UNCTC's extensive data base and policy recommendations remain in the U.N. archives and are a valuable resource to keep in mind.

In the past year, Boutras Ghali and his secretariat have reorganized the entire U.N. system while shifting the budget of the U.N. General Assembly away from economic and social cooperation. So-called "peacekeeping operations" are controlled by the small group of 5 powerful countries with a veto in the U.N. Security Council. But let's be very careful about what U.N. peacekeeping really means. In Somalia, U.N. peacekeeping means fighting over natural resources that are of interest to the transnational corporations. When the "peacekeeping" forces employ Third World soldiers instead of our own sons and daughters, then the potential for a powerful resistance movement in this country is very much diminished.

We, as citizens of the United States, have a global responsibility to question and challenge the lethal use of our military in interventions throughout the world. We must challenge its use to access the natural resources of other countries. We also have a responsibility to monitor events at the United Nations and among the Bretton Woods institutions, where our government plays a leading role. We cannot accept free trade or any other international agreements that are designed to supply the corporate world with cheap resources and cheap labor.

NAFTA'S NEW WORLD ECONOMY

Allowing corporations to exploit land, labor, and natural resources is equally the agenda behind NAFTA as well as GATT. Both strategies weaken the nation-state by eroding regulatory barriers to trade. For now, NAFTA is between Canada, the United States, and Mexico. However, one of NAFTA's most important clauses goes unreported in the mass media—its *accession clause*. We will soon notice that most other Latin American countries, not to mention New Zealand and several Asian nations, begin negotiating for access to NAFTA.

The accession clause significantly alters the economy of NAFTA. If you think about it as a regional agreement between the United States, Canada and Mexico, it's possible to anticipate some of the economic effects. With an active accession clause, NAFTA will have a much less predictable economic impact. Take the trade in sugar, for example. If NAFTA were limited to just Mexico, the United States, and Canada, we could anticipate the sugar trade to be displaced in the United States while Mexican farmers would experience the opportunity to develop that industry. With other countries signing on through the accession clause, however, sugar would be able to enter the North American market from almost anywhere in the world and compete with both the U.S. and Mexican sectors. Thus, the accession clause is the open door for corporations to locate anywhere in the world where costs will be lower and yet have easy access to the US market.

It is difficult to estimate the impact the globalized economy will have on jobs—although economists try. Using a global model, an econometric forecasting associate at the University of Pennsylvania projects that 1,400,000 U.S. jobs are vulnerable under GATT. The University of Massachusetts and Skidmore College came out with a study that said that under NAFTA up to 450,000 jobs are vulnerable. Their results are based on the fact that Mexico and other poor countries have a comparative advantage in low wages and non-enforced environmental regulations making it desirable for companies to relocate from more expensive places like the United States.

The Bush Administration's cheeriest economic projection suggested that only 64,000 jobs would be created by NAFTA. Analysts from the Economic Policy Institute examined the Bush Administration study and found two assumptions built into the projection that make it laughable. The first laugh comes from their assumption of full employment in the United States. The second laugh comes from their assumption that the Mexicans will become wealthy through trickle-down policies and begin to purchase American products that continue to be made *in the United States* by companies that haven't run south to Mexico and elsewhere.

The jobs that we're going to lose first are entry-level labor positions. We're talking about jobs held by women and people of color primarily: jobs in the garment industry, the food processing industry, and, to some extent, the automobile industry. Many more family farms in the United States will also fail as price supports and other policies are declared "trade barriers" by both the World Trade Organization and NAFTA's new bureaucracies.

Still an agrarian society, Mexico stands to lose some 2 to 12 million jobs in agriculture. About a third of its people still live off the land. Many of them live in what we would consider poverty, but many of them are growing enough food to feed themselves and their families. Under the deregulation that NAFTA brings to the Mexican agricultural sector, price supports for the food they eat—corn and beans—will be considered a non-tariff trade barrier to U.S. agribusiness. The Mexican government will be obliged to eliminate price supports to Mexican farmers, and the people who grow corn in that country will no longer be able to afford to do so. Instead, they will have to buy corn from the United States. (The world price for corn is far cheaper than the price that the government pays to corn farmers in Mexico today.)

Treating labor as just another tradable commodity, NAFTA paves the road toward massive urbanization. Mexico City, already one of the largest and arguably the most polluted cities in the world, will be inundated with new immigrants. The number of new jobs that might be created in industry will not approximate those that will be lost in agriculture. Our borders will feel new pressure as more Mexicans trying to compete with us for fewer jobs attempt to enter the United States illegally, because there is no reform of immigration policy in NAFTA.

SETTLING DISPUTES: GATT VS. NAFTA

The NAFTA text explicitly states that its rules will be "consistent" with the GATT although there are various differences. The most significant, probably, is a reversal of the burden of proof in a dispute although, as Zen Makuch of the Canadian Environmental Law Foundation has pointed out, "the onus of proof only plays a determinative role in legal cases that are evenly balanced, and trade disputes have not, to date, demonstrated such a fine balancing of evidence and law." Under GATT, a nation is considered guilty unless proven innocent; that is, the defendant must prove that its trade practice does not discriminate or otherwise violate the rules. Under NAFTA, the complainant must prove its case.

Switching the burden of proof could give some protection to nations legislating environmental, health and other social regulations that have trade effects—like those of Indonesia and Thailand which I mentioned earlier. For example, the GATT dispute-panel ruling against the Marine Mammal Protection Act might not have occurred under a NAFTA panel, where Mexico would have had to prove that this national law was not primarily a conservation measure.

However, because the United States, Mexico and Canada are all members of GATT, most of their disputes would also be eligible for resolution under the new World Trade Organization. The NAFTA text affirms that, in such cases, the complainant may choose either set of rules; logic suggests that most complainants would choose the GATT rules, thus switching the burden of proof back to the accused. Then again, NAFTA says that the defendant can insist upon a NAFTA dispute-resolution panel if the case involves facts regarding certain environmental, health and safety standards and certain international environmental agreements. But what are truly "facts"? Panels may be needed first to determine what is and is not factual—in aspects of policy that depend upon subjective judgements regarding risk, cause-and-effect, and so on.

Otherwise, a NAFTA dispute-settlement panel will consist of five members, not three as is traditional in the GATT. Also unlike GATT, a NAFTA panel "may" include experts specializing in fields other than trade; thus a nation may nominate environmentalists, lawyers, and "other" experts to the roster of potential panelists—although consulting this expertise is not obligatory. If both of the disputing parties agree, NAFTA will allow special scientific review boards to advise a panel on questions of fact. Separate provisions govern disputes over financial matters, intellectual property, agriculture, anti-dumping cases, and other cases brought to a NAFTA dispute proceeding. But just like GATT, NAFTA panels would be subject to strict confidentiality with no provision requiring public input.

In some ways, the NAFTA actually contradicts the GATT. For example, in NAFTA, Canadian farmers resisted negotiators' attempts to force them to discontinue managing the supply of dairy products, wheat and other crops. Obviously, if you manage the supply you can avoid the kinds of gluts that cause prices to fall below sustainable levels and, at the same time, you can generally better manage food safety and farm income. But the new rules for agriculture in the Uruguay Round agreement will force Canada to end this very successful program.

The new World Trade Organization will also inhibit the setting of national food safety laws that are stronger than those established by an international body controlled by the food industry! "Codex Alimentarius," for example, is a standard-setting agency of the U.N. Food and Agriculture Organization, in which the Nestlés Corporation alone has more personnel representing different countries' governments than has any one government! The U.S. delegation at recent Codex meetings included advisors from General Mills, Kraft, Purina, Pepsi-Cola, Coca-Cola, etc. In the name of the U.S. government, these food industry representatives negotiated international standards governing pesticides, sanitation, and food additives that do less to protect people than our own national laws prescribe. Outside democratic checks and balances, corporations are gaining control of rules and regulations that compromise the quality of our lives and the well being of the planet.

Under the Uruguay Round agreement, governments wishing to defend a national law that is stricter than what Codex has established must show that their domestic law is scientifically based and the least trade-restrictive way possible to achieve the stated goal. Innocent sounding enough, but can we believe the scientists employed by the R.J. Reynolds tobacco company when they claim that cigarette smoking does not cause cancer? Can we accept the notion that the less trade-restrictive policy of shipping beverages in recycled aluminum cans achieves the same environmental goal as the more trade-restrictive policy of returning and reusing bottles? I think these two examples show how this seemingly simple criteria—scientific justification and least trade restrictive—are subject to much judgement and political discretion. Yet, in the World Trade Organization, this judgement will be exercised by trade bureaucrats who view commercial activity as the end-all and be-all of international relations. Even the NAFTA, weak as it is, has a better approach to settling disputes than the Uruguay Round agreement of the GATT. Now we have to deal with both.

CLINTON'S "SIDE AGREEMENTS" LACK TEETH

In NAFTA, environmentalists and organized labor lobbied intensively for side agreements which would include citizens in the dispute-settlement process, provide adjustment for displaced workers, ensure the right to organize and strike, preserve higher standards and clean up the toxic conditions in the unregulated industrial zones along the U.S.-Mexican border, called the *maquiladoras*. Lack of regulations in these zones has resulted in well-documented "free trade atrocities," as in the cases of babies being born without brains. In total disregard for human life, companies dump their wastes right into the streets—*with children playing in them!* The water supply that irrigates the agriculture belt along California and Texas is at risk, too, because it draws from the same untreated source. Clinton's side agreements, however, achieve none of these goals although they do set up bureaucratic systems where complaints can be formally lodged.

After a year of secret negotiations, the Clinton side agreements were finally made public. Critics found them weak. Some pointed out that they do not begin to fix major problems in the original text such as the emphasis on agricultural concentration or guarantees of undiminished energy exports. Others remembered the long list of Clinton's campaign promises—not the least of which was protection for national and state laws setting higher standards than those of the international bureaucracies. Of all the Clinton promises, however, the three new agreements address only the creation of trinational labor and environmental commissions and reiterate the original NAFTA terms regarding sudden gluts of imports, called "surges."

Some critics would have been satisfied with the supplemental agreements if they were ensured a dispute-settlement mechanism with "teeth." But the teeth are missing. Indeed, according to the *Journal of Commerce*, Mexico's chief NAFTA negotiator Jaime Serra Puche told the Mexican Senate not to worry about the threat of fines and trade sanctions resulting from the supplemental agreements. The trilateral commissions' powers are limited, he said on August 17, 1993, and the "exceedingly long" dispute-resolution process "makes it very improbable that the stage of sanctions could be reached." Furthermore, the maximum penalty would be a fine or suspension of benefits worth $20 million—peanuts to any of the three governments.

The text also carefully circumscribes which laws are subject to the jurisdiction of the trilateral commissions. Only those environmental laws affecting the production of tradable goods and services are at stake; laws whose "primary purpose" is natural resource management are explicitly excluded. Likewise, labor laws guaranteeing the right to freely associate and organize, to bargain collectively, and to strike are excluded; only "mutually recognized" laws and regulations addressing workplace health and safety, a minimum wage, and child labor are subject to dispute resolution. Neither commission may refer complaints—even those meeting all criteria—to a dispute-resolution panel unless two of the three countries' governments agree.

SCRAPS FOR THE PUBLIC

A careful reading shows that the three supplemental agreements altogether create ten new bureaucracies with responsibilities that are largely informational. Words like "consider," "consult," "report," "recommend," "promote," and "work toward" abound. And the entire side agreement on surges is, according to the three governments' official summary, merely an "Understanding" that "confirms the ... effective use of Chapter Eight of the NAFTA" by establishing a Working Group on Emergency Action which "may make recommendations" to the governing bodies created by the NAFTA text itself.

On the other hand, an argument can be made that the side agreements enable a degree of accessibility. Working groups, advisory boards and other channels of communication are established. Individual citizens may bring complaints to the environmental commission—although not to the labor commission where only national governments have standing. If a dispute panel is convened, panelists may have expertise in fields other than trade policy and a panel may, if all parties agree, summon environmental, labor, and other expertise.

In the context of accessibility, it is notable that the Clinton Administration chose to appeal and succeeded in overturning a federal judge's ruling that the National Environmental Policy Act requires an Environmental Impact Statement to be conducted on NAFTA. A Mexican coalition of labor, peasant and environmental groups, also filed its own request for an evaluation of the environmental impact of NAFTA on Mexico, citing their Constitutional guarantees of "the right to health, the conservation of productive resources and the care of ecosystems and natural resources" and other national laws. It will require all the wit and resources of labor and environmental advocates to take advantage of the NAFTA commissions and test their usefulness as instruments of justice.

ORGANIZING & RESISTANCE

Armed peasants in Chiapas, a Southern state of Mexico, denounced NAFTA as "a death sentence for the indigenous people." Chief among their demands are land reform and democracy, quite the opposite of NAFTA and its agriculture policy. In a letter published in Mexican newspapers, the Zapatista National Liberation Army explained that, a "handful of businesses, one of which is the state of Mexico, take all the wealth out of Chiapas leaving behind... ecological destruction, agricultural scraps, hyperinflation, alcoholism, prostitution, and poverty." In another letter addressed to President Clinton and the people of the United States, the Zapatistas implored us, "do not stain your hands with our blood by allowing yourselves to be the accomplices of the Mexican government."

In the spirit of alternative cooperative relations on our continent, Mexicans, Canadians, and U.S. activists organized numerous tri-national meetings throughout the NAFTA negotiations. For example, the corn farmers from the three countries sat down and hammered out a policy on corn that would have satisfied all the farmers although it was ignored by government negotiators. Similarly, dairy farmers, timber workers, auto workers, environmental workers, and garment workers have had trilateral meetings of this sort.

A number of innovative proposals for using international agreements go beyond trade—which is essentially a commercial agreement—and bring in a comprehensive range of other issues. Cuauhtémoc Cárdenas, leader of the opposition party in Mexico, who many people believe won the last election except that it was stolen from him by fraud, has written an impressive and simple five-page paper outlining ten different items that would go into a fair *continental initiative* as he calls it—not a trade agreement, but a continental initiative.

Others are developing interesting ideas about technology and development. Herman Daly, an economist who just retired from the World Bank, has proposed a number of specific criteria for using technology to ensure sustainable development. Appropriate technology, Daly argues, would harvest renewable resources and create wastes at a rate no greater than the earth can replenish and assimilate them. The Green Forum (Philippines) argues that gross domestic product (GDP) only measures the wealth of corporations, whereas household income measures the welfare of the community. The Green Forum also incorporates ecological assets into its concept of "Community Networth." By substituting "ecological zones" for arbitrary political districts, it becomes easier to calculate the ecological costs of production that would be paid to a community by the corporations that exploit their natural resources.

Non-governmental groups at the Earth Summit in Rio de Janeiro negotiated among themselves about 40 "alternative treaties" (see the Econet conference, "unced.treaties") that cover a whole range of issues regarding international development and a fair world order. I worked on the one that addressed fair trade in very specific terms.

Unfortunately, implementing these and other proposals for fair international policies will be nearly impossible unless there is fundamental change in the structure of the Bretton Woods institutions to make them democratic, accessible, and accountable with economic opportunity and ecological economics balanced in a planetary approach to social development. The new World Trade Organization is a step in the wrong direction. So too are the shifts in the United Nations' budget from the General Assembly to the Security Council.

In 1994 and 1995, the governments of the world will celebrate the 50th anniversary of Bretton Woods and the U.N. respectively. Simultaneously, non-governmental organizations are planning protests against the dominant "predatory" mode of development—as Third World groups have called this system—and planning alternative conferences to design policies and institutions that can build a new community-based world order for the coming century. Be there!

Global Village or Global Pillage?
Resistance to Top-Down Globalization
By Jeremy Brecher

For most of the world's people, the "New World Economy" is a disaster that has already happened. Those it hurts can't escape it. But neither can they afford to accept it. So many are now seeking ways to reshape it.

When I first started writing about the destructive effects of globalization some three years ago, the North American Free Trade Agreement was widely regarded as a done deal. The near defeat of NAFTA reveals pervasive popular doubt about the wisdom of an unregulated international market. The struggle against NAFTA represented the first major effort by Americans who have been hurt by global economic integration to do something about it. Like many mass movements, it included contradictory forces, such as the Mexico-bashing bigotry of Pat Buchanan, the populist grandstanding of Ross Perot and the nationalistic protectionism of some in the labor movement.

But other elements of the struggle against NAFTA prefigure a movement that could radically reshape the New World Economy. Out of their own experiences and observations, millions of Americans have constructed a new paradigm for understanding the global economy. Poor and working people in large numbers have recognized that NAFTA is not primarily about trade; it is about the ability of capital to move without regard to national borders. Capital mobility, not trade, is bringing about the "giant sucking sound" of jobs going South.

For the first time in many years, substantial numbers of people mobilized to act on broad class interests. I haven't seen a movement for years in which so many people at the grass roots took their own initiative. Typical was the unexpectedly large, predominantly blue-collar anti-NAFTA rally in New Haven, where a labor leader told me, "We didn't turn these people out."

THE NEW GLOBAL PILLAGE

NAFTA became a symbol for an accumulation of fears and angers regarding the place of working people in the New World Economy. The North American economic integration that NAFTA was intended to facilitate is only one aspect of a rapid and momentous historical transformation from a system of national economies toward an integrated global economy. New information, communication, transportation, and manufacturing technologies, combined with tariff reductions, have made it possible to coordinate production, commerce, and finance on a world scale. Since 1983, the rate of world foreign direct investment has grown four times as fast as world output.

This transformation has had devastating consequences. They may be summarized as the "seven danger signals" of cancerous, out-of-control globalization:

Race to the bottom. The recent quantum leap in the ability of transnational corporations to relocate their facilities around the world in effect makes all workers, communities, and countries competitors for these corporations' favor. The consequence is a "race to the bottom" in which wages and social and environmental conditions tend to fall to the level of the most desperate. This dynamic underlies U.S. deindustrialization, declining real wages, eradication of job security, and downward pressure on social spending and investment; it is also largely responsible for the migration of low-wage, environmentally destructive industries to poor countries like Mexico and China.

Global stagnation. As each workforce, community, or country seeks to become more competitive by reducing its wages and its social and environmental overheads, the result is a general downward spiral in incomes and social and material infrastructures. Lower wages and reduced public spending mean less buying power, leading to stagnation, recession, and unemployment. This dynamic is aggravated by the accumulation of debt; national economies in poor countries and even in the United States become geared to debt repayment at the expense of consumption, investment, and development. The downward fall is reflected in the slowing of global GNP growth from almost 5 percent per year in the period 1948-1973 to only half that in the period 1974-1989 and to a mere crawl since then.

Polarization of haves and have-nots. As a result of globalization, the gap between rich and poor is increasing both within and between countries around the world. Poor U.S. communities boast world-class unemployment and infant mortality. Meanwhile, tens of billions of dollars a year flow from poor to rich regions of the world, in the form of debt repayment and capital flight.

Loss of democratic control. National governments have lost much of their power to control their own economies. The ability of countries to apply socialist or even Keynesian techniques in pursuit of development, full employment, or other national economic goals has been undermined by the power of capital to pick up and leave. Governmental economic power has been further weakened throughout the world by neo-liberal political movements that have dismantled government institutions for regulating national economies. Globalization has reduced the power of individuals and communities to shape their destinies.

Walter Wriston, former chairman of Citicorp, recently boasted of how "200,000 monitors in trading rooms all over the world" now conduct "a kind of global plebiscite on the monetary and fiscal policies of the governments issuing currency ... There is no way for a nation to opt out." Wriston recalls the election of "ardent socialist" Francois Mitterand in 1981. "The market took one look at his policies and within six months the capital flight forced him to reverse course."

Unfettered transnational corporations. Transnationals have become the world's most powerful economic actors, yet there are no international equivalents to the national antitrust, consumer protection and other laws that provide a degree of corporate accountability.

Unaccountable global institutions. The loss of national economic control has been accompanied by a growing concentration of unaccountable power in international institutions like the IMF, the World Bank, and the GATT. For poor countries, foreign control has been formalized in the World Bank's "Structural Adjustment Plans," but IMF decisions and GATT rules affect the economic growth rates of all countries. The decisions of these institutions also have an enormous impact on the global ecology.

Global conflict. Economic globalization is producing chaotic and destructive rivalries. In a swirl of self-contradictory strategies, major powers and transnationals use global institutions like GATT to impose open markets on their rivals; they pursue trade wars against one other; and they try to construct competing regional blocs like the European Union and NAFTA. In past eras, such rivalries have ultimately led to world war.

In sum, the result of unregulated globalization has been the pillage of the planet and its peoples.

TRANSNATIONAL ECONOMIC PROGRAMS

What are the alternatives to destructive globalization? The right offers racism and nationalism. Conventional protectionism offers no solution. Globalization has also intellectually disarmed the left and rendered national left programs counterproductive. Jimmy Carter's sharp turn to the right in 1978; Francois Mitterand's rapid abandonment of his radical program; the acceptance of deregulation, privatization, and trade liberalization by poor countries from India to Mexico; and even the decision of Eastern European elites to abandon Communism—all reflect in part the failure of national left policies.

But the beginnings of a new approach emerged from the anti-NAFTA movement itself. Rather than advocate protectionism—keeping foreign products out—many NAFTA opponents urged policies that would raise environmental, labor and social standards in Mexico, so that those standards would not drag down those in the United States and Canada. This approach implied that people in different countries have common interests in raising the conditions of those at the bottom.

Indeed, the struggle against NAFTA generated new transnational networks based on such common interests. A North American Worker-to-Worker Network links grass-roots labor activists in Mexico, the United States and Canada via conferences, tours, solidarity support, and a newsletter. Mujer a Mujer similarly links women's groups. The Highlander Center, Southerners for Economic Justice, the Tennessee Industrial Renewal Network, and a number of unions have organized meetings and tours to bring together Mexican and U.S. workers. There are similar networks in other parts of the world, such as the People's Plan 21 in the Asian-Pacific and Central American regions and the Third World Network in Malaysia.

These new networks are developing transnational programs to counter the effects of global economic restructuring. Representatives from environmental, labor, religious, consumer and farm groups from Mexico, the United States and Canada have drawn up "A Just and Sustainable Trade and Development Initiative for North America." A parallel synthesis, "From Global Pillage to Global Village," has been endorsed by more than sixty grass-roots organizations. Related proposals by the Third World Network have recently been published as "Toward a New North-South Economic Dialogue."

Differing in emphasis and details, these emerging alternative programs are important not only because of the solutions they propose, but also because those solutions have emerged from a dialogue rooted in such a diversity of groups and experiences. Some require implementation by national policy; some by international agreement; some can be implemented by transnational citizen action. Taken together, they provide what might be described as "seven prescriptions" for the seven danger signals of the unregulated global economy:

International rights and standards. To prevent competition from resulting in a "race to the bottom," several of these groups want to establish minimum human, labor, and environmental rights and standards, as the European Union's "social charter" was designed to do. The International Metalworkers Federation recently proposed a ten-point "World Social Charter," which could be incorporated into GATT.

"A Just and Sustainable Trade and Development Initiative for North America" spells out in some detail an alternative to NAFTA that would protect human and worker rights, encourage workers' income to rise in step with productivity and establish continental environmental rights, such as the right to a toxics-free workplace and community. Enforcement agencies would be accessible to citizens and could levy fines against parties guilty of violations. The initiative especially emphasizes the rights of immigrants. Activists from non-governmental organizations in all three countries have proposed a citizen's commission to monitor human, labor and environmental effects of trade and investment.

Upward spiral. In the past, government monetary and fiscal policy, combined with minimum wages, welfare state programs, collective bargaining and other means of raising the purchasing power of have-nots, did much to counter recession and stagnation within national economies. Similar measures are now required at international levels to counter the tendency toward a downward spiral of inadequate demand in the global economy. The Third World Network calls on the IMF and World bank to replace their ruinous structural adjustment plans with policies that "meet the broad goals of development ... rather than the narrower goal of satisfying the needs of creditors." It also demands a reduction of developing countries' debt. "A Just and Sustainable Trade and Development Initiative" proposes that the remaining debt service be paid in local currency into a democratically administered development fund. Reversing the downward spiral also ultimately requires a "global Keynesianism" in which international institutions support, rather than discourage, national full-employment policies.

An upward spiral also requires rising income for those at the bottom—something that can be encouraged by international labor solidarity. Experiments in cross-border organizing by U.S. unions like the Amalgamated Clothing and Textile Workers and the United Electrical Workers, in cooperation with independent unions in Mexico, aim to defeat Transnationals' whipsawing by improving the wages and conditions of Mexican workers.

Redistribution from haves to have-nots. "A Just and Sustainable Trade and Development Initiative" calls for "compensatory financing" to correct growing gaps between rich and poor. A model would be the European Union funds that promote development in its poorer members. The Third World Network calls for commodity agreements to correct the inequities in the South's terms of trade. It also stresses the need to continue preferential treatment for the South in GATT and in intellectual property protection rules.

Strengthened democracy. NAFTA, GATT and similar agreements should not be used—as they now can be—to preempt the right of localities, states, provinces and countries to establish effective labor, health, safety and environmental standards that are higher than the guaranteed minimum in international agreements. Above all, democratization requires a new opportunity for people at the bottom to participate in shaping their destiny.

Codes of Conduct for Transnational Corporations. Several transnational grass-roots groups call for codes of conduct that would, for example, require corporations to report investment intentions; disclose the hazardous materials they import; ban employment of children; forbid discharge of pollutants; require advance notification and severance pay when operations are terminated; and prohibit company interference with union organizing. United Nations discussions on such a code, long stymied by U.S. hostility, should be revived.

While the ultimate goal is to have such codes implemented by agreements among governments, global public pressure and cross-border organizing can begin to enforce them. The Coalition for Justice in the Maquiladoras, for example, a coalition of religious, environmental, labor, Latino and women's organizations in Mexico and the United States, has issued a code of conduct for U.S. corporations in Mexico and has used "corporate campaign" techniques to pressure them to abide by its labor and environmental provisions.

Reform of international institutions. Citizens should call on the United Nations to convene a second Earth Summit focusing on democratizing the IMF and the World Bank, and consider formation of new institutions to promote equitable, sustainable and participatory development. International citizen campaigns, perhaps modeled on the Nestlé boycott and the campaign against World Bank-funded destruction of the Amazon, could spotlight these institutions.

Multiple-level regulation. In place of rivalry among countries and regions, such programs imply a system of democratically controlled public institutions at every level, from global to local.

GLOBALIZATION FROM BELOW

These proposals provide no short-term panacea; they are objectives to organize around. The New World Economy is not going to vanish from the political agenda. Neither will the passions and political forces aroused by the NAFTA debate. Many of the same issues will resurface in connection with the Asia-Pacific Economic Cooperation Forum and with GATT. As the fiftieth anniversaries of the IMF and World Bank approach, calls for their reform are being sounded all over the world.

The struggle against NAFTA has shown that those harmed by the New World Economy need not be passive victims. Many politicians were unprepared for the strength of the anti-NAFTA movement because it represented an eruption into the political arena of people who have long been demobilized. But to influence their economic destinies effectively, they need a movement that provides an alternative the Ross Perots and Pat Buchanans. Such a movement must act on the understanding that the unregulated globalization of capital is really a worldwide attack of the haves on the have-nots. And it must bring that understanding to bear on every affected issue, from local layoffs to the world environment. "From Global Pillage to Global Village" suggests a vision to guide such a movement:

> The internationalization of capital, production and labor is now being followed by the internationalization of peoples' movements and organizations. Building peoples' international organizations and solidarity will be our revolution from within: a civil society without borders. This internationalism or "globalization from below" will be the foundation for turning the global pillage into a participatory and sustainable global village.

More Information

• INSTITUTE for AGRICULTURE & TRADE POLICY
IATP was organized in 1986 to alert the public to the dangers encoded in free trade and tariff agreements. From monitoring GATT, NAFTA, and UNCED developments to providing "win-win" solutions to trade conflicts, IATP is invaluable to all people working for a balanced, sustainable future.
**1313 Fifth St. SE #303, Minneapolis, MN 55414
Tel. 612-379-5980 Fax. 612-379-5982 E-mail. igc.iatp**

**• ZAPATISTAS:
SPREADING HOPE FOR GRASSROOTS CHANGE**
This pamphlet features the original declarations of the Zapatista insurgents in Chiapas, Mexico, the incisive on-site reporting of Marc Cooper, plus solidarity and resistance notes by Barbara Pillsbury and Hannah Holm. Order your copy from Open Media:
P.O. Box 2726, Westfield, NJ 07091 Tel. (908) 789-9608

• MEXICO-US DIALOGOS
Mexico-US Dialogos was founded in 1988 as a program to promote an ongoing interchange between social constituencies in the United States and Mexico directly affected by economic integration. An Information resource for social organizations in both countries. Contact: Dave Brooks
**103 Washington Street, Suite 8, NYC 10006
Tel. 212-233-0155 Fax. 212-233-0238
E-mail. dialogos@igc.apc.org**

• PUBLIC CITIZEN
Public Citizen is a non-profit organization that fights for consumer rights in the marketplace, for a healthy environment and workplace, for clean and safe energy resources, and for corporate and government accountability. Their research and activism are at the center of anti-GATT and anti-NAFTA movements. Contact:
**215 Pennsylvania Ave SE, Wash., D.C. 20003
Tel. 202-546-4996 Fax. 202-547-7392 E-Mail. pcctw@igc.apc.org**

• CITIZENS TRADE CAMPAIGN
CTC is a national coalition of consumer, environmental, labor, family farm, religious, and other civic groups promoting a citizens' agenda in U.S. trade policy. Engaging 60 national groups and 45 million U.S. citizens, CTC lobbies Congress as a coalition against GATT and NAFTA. For more information contact:
600 Maryland Ave, SW, Wash., D.C. 20024 Tel. 202-554-1102

• CENTER FOR POPULAR ECONOMICS
CPE offers training workshops/programs for community and labor organizers who have not had formal economics training. Classes are designed to de-mystify economics, and provide a framework for understanding the economy and alternatives to mainstream and conservative analyses. For publications, contact:
P.O. Box 7852, Amherst, MA 01004 Tel: (413) 545-0743

• DOLLARS AND SENSE MAGAZINE
D&S offers progressive economic analysis accessible to people with no formal training. They publish annual editions of *Real World Macro*, an anthology of *D&S* articles organized in a textbook format. 10 issues a year. Individual $22.95/yr; $39/2yrs. Institution: $42/yr; $84/2yrs.
One Summer Street, Somerville, MA 02143 Tel. (617) 628-8411

• GOVERNMENT ACCOUNTABILITY PROJECT
A non-profit organization, GAP provides legal and advocacy assistance to concerned citizens who witness dangerous, illegal, or environmentally unsound practices in their workplaces and communities and choose to "blow the whistle." For a $35 annual subscription to *Bridging The Gap*, or a catalog of titles, contact:
**810 First Street NE, Suite 630, Washington, D.C. 20002-3633
Tel. 202-408-0034 Fax. 202-408-9855**